DIY Mandala

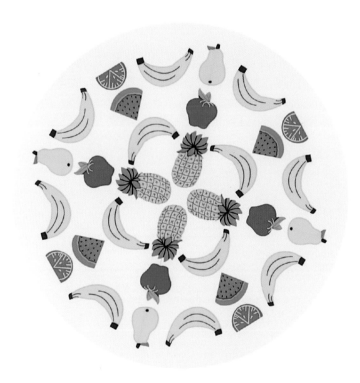

This library edition published in 2017 by Walter Foster Jr.,
an imprint of The Quarto Group
6 Orchard Road, Suite 100
Lake Forest, CA 92630

Acquiring & Project Editor: Stephanie Carbajal
Page Layout: Andrea Miller
Artwork and photographs on pages 4–21 and pages 98–127 © 2016 Louise Gale.
Artwork and photographs on pages 22–41 © 2016 Andrea Thompson. Artwork and
photographs on pages 42–69 © 2016 Marisa Edghill. Artwork and photographs on
pages 70–97 © 2016 Alyssa Stokes.

Distributed in the United States and Canada by
Lerner Publisher Services
241 First Avenue North
Minneapolis, MN 55401 U.S.A.
www.lernerbooks.com

First Library Edition

Library of Congress Cataloging-in-Publication Data

Names: Gale, Louise. Mandala basics.
Title: DIY mandala.
Other titles: Mandala for the inspired artist.
Description: First library edition. | Lake Forest, CA : Walter Foster
    Publishing, an imprint of The Quarto Group, 2017. | Includes
    bibliographical references and index. | Audience: Ages 10+.
Identifiers: LCCN 2017011683 | ISBN 9781942875284 (hardcover : alk. paper)
Subjects: LCSH: Handicraft. | Mandala-- Miscellanea.
Classification: LCC TT157 .M3475 2017 | DDC 745.5-- dc23
LC record available at https://lccn.loc.gov/2017011683

Printed in USA
9 8 7 6 5 4 3 2 1

TABLE OF CONTENTS

MANDALA BASICS

LOUISE GALE

MANDALA BASICS

WHAT IS A MANDALA?

Mandala comes from the Sanskrit language, loosely meaning "circle." They represent the wholeness of the universe.

Most mandalas are circular with different patterns that radiate outward. They usually contain 8 or 12 symmetrical sections.

The purpose and design of any mandala is up to the creator. It can be simple, or very detailed and complex, filled with layers of motifs; or it might be an intricate creation of colored sand.

I like to think of a mandala as a circle that tells a story about who we are, or the world around us. Mandalas are personal and unique, and can be both inspirational and therapeutic.

HAND-DRAWN MANDALA USING THE 8-POINT STRUCTURE AND DEVELOPING INTO 12 MOTIFS AROUND THE EDGE

WHERE DO MANDALAS COME FROM?

The circle is the most natural form known to humankind. Mandalas can be seen in all aspects of life—the Earth, the moon, and the sun, as well as through circles of friends, family, and communities. Mandalas are found on large and small scales, from the rotational patterns of planets to the intricate, geometric pattern of a flower.

6

Mandalas are specifically associated with traditional Hindu, Tibetan, and Buddhist artwork, but they are also found in other world traditions—the rose windows of Gothic cathedrals, Native American dream catchers and labyrinths, Aboriginal art, and Aztec sunstones, among many others.

Many buildings have also been built using mandalic patterns, often for spiritual purposes, but also as a geometric way to ensure balance and harmony in the architecture or design.

HOW ARE MANDALAS STRUCTURED?

Mandalas have one identifiable center point that different symbols, shapes, and patterns spread from—these vary from culture to culture.

The basic form of a traditional mandala is a square with four "gates" containing a circle. Each gate is in the general shape of a T.

Mandala patterns on a church in Jerez, Spain

Sri Yantra
Mandala

Some traditions portray images of gods and goddesses, some use color and shape, and others use natural objects. Although each culture may use different symbols, all mandalas describe the same cosmos, which symbolizes unity and harmony for all.

Mandalas can be created with a 4-point, 8-point, or 12-point structure using spirals, concentric circles, and other recognizable formations. You can draw them freehand or use a ruler, protractor, and compass to measure sections and create concentric circles. Each mandala design can be structured in a different way, and many consist of various mathematical combinations, themes, or patterns. (See pages 12–18 for more details on drawing your own mandalas.)

A MANDALA?

You can use a variety of materials to create mandalas, such as a black pen, paint, collage, pressed flowers, and more! Mandalas can be doodled in your sketchbook, painted on paper, or created as detailed, mixed media masterpieces. You can even create them digitally on the computer or paint on stones and other circular objects, such as old CDs or vinyl records.

Creating temporary mandalas is also a wonderful way to create with and connect to nature. You can use found objects from nature, such as petals and leaves, colored sand, or shells.

PRESSED FLOWER MANDALA

HOW ARE MANDALAS USED?

Mandalas have traditionally been used by Buddhists, Hindus, Tibetans, and Native Americans in prayer, meditation, and healing. For example, Tibetan monks use mandalas as a form of meditation—the observer focuses and meditates on the special symbolic meaning within the mandala, considering the entire world through it.

Tibetan monks also create intricate colored sand mandalas, in which the focus is on the act of carefully creating the mandala; once completed, a ceremony is performed in which the sand is poured away.

In the early twentieth century, Swiss psychiatrist and psychotherapist Carl Jung noticed how mandala making was used by many cultures to represent wholeness and healing through ritual. In his book *Man and His Symbols* (1968), Jung saw this process as a way to facilitate healing through creating art. As a result of this discovery, the creation of mandalas is used frequently today in art therapy and meditation.

8

WHAT ARE THE BENEFITS OF MAKING MANDALAS?

The process of making mandalas centers the mind and produces a sense of peace and calmness. Anyone can use mandalas as a tool for meditation, relaxation, and introspection. The process can take as little as two minutes to doodle in a sketchbook or up to several hours to paint one full of layers, colors, and depth on a canvas.

While there doesn't necessarily need to be meaning behind your mandalas, you may find symbols that are meaningful to you or that simply convey the beauty in the world. Coloring mandalas is also a great way to relax. Even those who may not want to create a mandala from scratch can still benefit from the healing and reflective process of coloring.

Mandala making is a mindful process, and within this book you will discover tools, techniques, and opportunities to create beautiful mandala works of art.

TIBETAN MANDALA

DRAWING &
COLORING MANDALAS

LOUISE GALE

11

DRAWING MANDALAS

LOOKING FOR INSPIRATION

Mandala inspiration is all around us! It's in our homes, in architecture designs, and—most abundantly—in nature. Look for the mandalas around you, and notice the beautiful designs, motifs, and patterns in fabric designs, candle holders, a slice of lemon, the center of a flower, or a delicate urchin on the beach.

GETTING STARTED

Before you begin your mandala, create a space for yourself that is comfortable, inspiring and free of distraction. The process of drawing or coloring a mandala can be a calming and meditative experience, so be mindful of enjoying the moment. There are many different ways to approach drawing a mandala. In this introduction, you'll find a simple doodling and motif exercise, a freehand approach, and a structured approach—all of which you can use as a foundation for your mandala designs. Whether you strive for structure or love to doodle, you will find endless joy in drawing and coloring many different types of mandalas!

MATERIALS
- Compass and pencil
- Protractor
- Ruler
- Black pen
- Eraser
- Colored pens, pencils, or crayons

DOODLE IN A CIRCLE

Doodling inside a circle is a great way to get started with mandala making. It's all about exploring the possibilities inside a simple circle, so you can start small and expand your circles and the number of motif designs as you become more confident.

Use a compass to draw a small circle (about 4" in diameter), or you can trace a small dish or plate. Draw a simple shape inside, such as a flower, a swirl, lines bursting from the center, or repeated petals. Doodle a variety of circles to help loosen you up. Pay attention to the types of motifs or shapes that you are drawn to the most as you doodle.

Here are some of my examples:

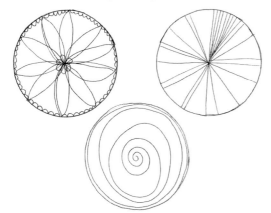

IDENTIFYING & BUILDING YOUR OWN UNIQUE MOTIFS

When you closely study more detailed mandalas, you'll start to identify the beautiful motifs the creator has used. If you are very new to drawing mandalas, study a few of your favorite mandala images and pull out your favorite motifs for inspiration. Then start a page in your sketchbook of your own unique doodles and motifs. Below are some of my favorite doodles, which I use in many of my own mandalas.

Photocopy or trace over this circle; then doodle inside to warm up
or use it as a template for your designs.

GROW A MANDALA

This is a completely loose and freeing way to create a doodled mandala. Start by drawing one motif in the center of your page, such as a dot or a flower. Then "grow" the mandala outward repeating your favorite icons or motifs around the central focal point. For example, if you start with a flower that has eight petals, repeat your next motif in the spaces between the petals eight times and so on.

CREATE A STRUCTURED MANDALA

Creating a structured mandala is a great way to guide your mandala creations if doodling freehand does not come easily at first. As with all mandala creations, there are endless possibilities for design and structure, so enjoy exploring and creating your own unique mandalas. Soon you will soon find a flow and style that you love.

ARTIST'S TIP

Divide 360 by the number of sections you want in your mandala. The result is the number of degrees to mark your points with using your protractor.

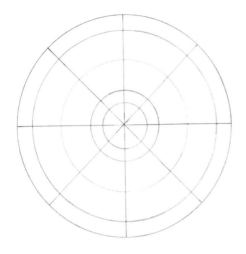

STEP 1

Draw a circle with your compass and pencil. Then line up a protractor to mark the number of points you would like to create around the circle. For an eight-point mandala, the points will be separated by 45 degrees around the protractor (360/8=45). Use a ruler to join the points, creating eight equal sections. Then use the compass to draw a series of concentric circles, varying the gap size. I added four circles.

STEP 2

Now you're ready to start drawing your mandala in pen. Starting at the center, choose one motif to repeat in each of the eight sections within that circle. You can draw on the lines themselves or in the space between.

STEP 3

Move outward through each section, connecting the points where the lines meet to create a new motif, so the design flows together. In the second circle, I drew a lotus petal, connecting the edges of the petal with the tip of the central motif. In the third circle, I drew larger petals again connecting the edges with the previous motif.

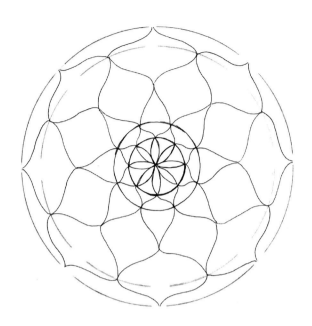

STEP 4
Now you have the base of your mandala and can add more detail. You can keep all of your original grid lines in place, or you can erase some of them to open up the design. I erased all of the straight lines and the central circle.

STEP 5
Add lines and other motifs to your mandala. Let your intuition guide you as you draw and add beautiful detail. When you're done, erase any remaining pencil lines.

ARTIST'S TIP
Photocopy your mandalas, and experiment with different color combinations using the color theory section.

MY MOTIFS

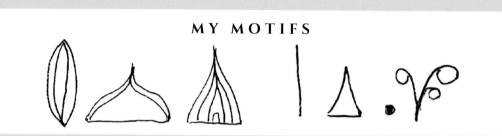

18

COLORING MANDALAS

Coloring mandalas can be very therapeutic. Color is a personal choice, so when you're selecting your palette, tap into your intuition to pick those that are speaking to you on that particular day. For a little more inspiration, follow these color theory basics to create harmony in your artwork.

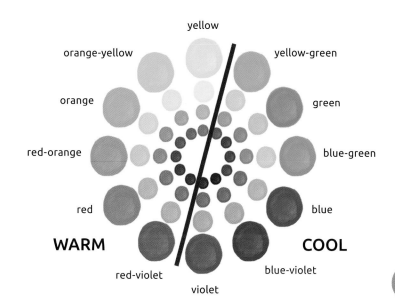

yellow

orange-yellow

yellow-green

orange

green

red-orange

blue-green

red

blue

WARM

COOL

blue-violet

red-violet

violet

THE COLOR WHEEL
The color wheel is a great tool for artists and designers. You can use this as a resource to get a feel for how color works as you select color combinations for your mandala artwork.

WARM & COOL COLORS
The color wheel is divided into warm and cool colors. Using either a warm or cool palette will create harmony in your artwork.

MONOCHROMATIC
If you have a favorite color, create a mandala in shades of that color. Monochromatic color schemes can be calming or energetic, depending on which side of the color wheel you use.

COMPLEMENTARY COLORS
Complementary colors sit directly opposite each other on the color wheel. They balance each other perfectly and make each other "pop."

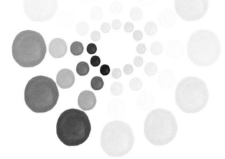

ANALOGOUS COLORS
An analogous color scheme uses three colors that sit beside each other on the color wheel. This kind of color scheme is very harmonizing.

ARTIST'S TIP
Explore and collect your own favorite color palette combinations. Take your camera on a walk and photograph colors that inspire unique palettes and combinations for your artwork.

Photocopy this template; then choose a color scheme, and color in this mandala with colored pencils, pens, or markers.

DRAWING & COLORING MANDALAS

WATERCOLOR MANDALAS

ANDREA THOMPSON

PETAL MANDALA

You can use any colors to paint this pretty petal mandala! By varying the placement of the colors, you can achieve a completely different feel in your mandala. I like to place complementary colors next to each other to make the petal shapes really stand out.

24

MATERIALS
- Watercolor paper
- Watercolor paints
- Small watercolor brush
- White gel pen
- Compass with a hard-lead pencil
- Ruler or straight edge

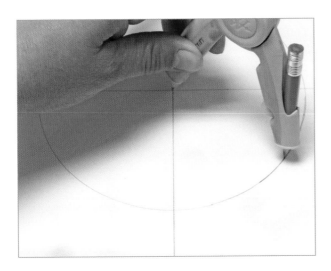

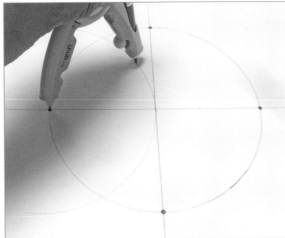

STEP 1

Measure the length and width of your paper to find the center. Lightly draw a horizontal and a vertical line through the center. Holding the point of your compass where the lines intersect, lightly draw a circle that is large enough to reach about an inch from both edges.

STEP 2

Keeping your compass open to the same distance, hold the point where the circle intersects with the horizontal and verticals lines (see the red dots in the photo), and lightly draw four more circles.

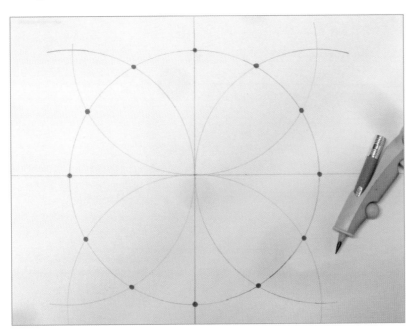

STEP 3

Holding the point of the compass on the new points you have made, (see the red dots in the photo), lightly draw eight more circles. You can now see petal shapes and are ready to start painting! If you have drawn the lines lightly with a hard-lead pencil, there is no need to erase any lines; the marks will not show through in the final piece and shouldn't bleed with the addition of watercolors.

STEP 4

Paint the innermost petals red. Then paint the second-to-last row of petals with yellow. (Using more pigment at the innermost tip, and blending out with just water at the outer tip will create a nice gradient.)

ARTIST'S TIP

Skipping the petals in between allows the red paint to dry, so the colors won't bleed into each other.

STEP 5

Paint the in-between petals with yellow, followed by green, and ending with blue. While the paint is wet, blend the three colors together with a damp brush. Then mix red and blue to create a violet mix, and paint the outermost petals

STEP 6
Add a second layer of paint, and then splatter a bit of violet paint around the edges of the mandala by tapping your brush above the paper.

STEP 7
Use a white gel pen to outline the center red flower and draw leafy designs in the green petals.

STEP 8
Draw tiny stems of leaves in the yellow petals, and paint a tiny touch of green in the leaves. To finish, draw scallops in a feathery doodle in the violet petals.

TRY SOMETHING DIFFERENT

Vary the types of doodles you place over your watercolors for countless
variations of this one simple mandala design!

MONOCHROMATIC MANDALA

This simple mandala can take on a different look depending on the color you choose and how much detail you add at the end. Sometimes I add shading with pencil, sometimes I add more detail, and sometimes I add less detail—only stop when the piece "feels" done to you!

MATERIALS
- Watercolor paper
- Watercolor paints
- Small watercolor brush
- Compass with a hard lead pencil
- Ruler or straight edge

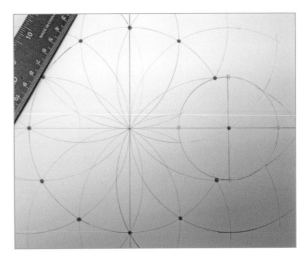

STEP 1
Follow steps 1 through 3 on page 25, but make the initial circle a little smaller. Next adjust the opening of the compass to the distance between two dots, and draw a small circle at the east point.

STEP 2
Draw a vertical and horizontal line in the small circle using a ruler or straight edge. Note the four yellow points for step 3.

STEP 3
Keep your compass at the same measurement, and draw four circles, starting with the four yellow points shown in step 2. Continue on, drawing eight more circles just as you did with the larger mandala. Repeat to create a small petal mandala at the north, south, and west points.

STEP 4
Pick any paint color—I chose red—
and paint the petals with a light
watercolor wash.

STEP 5
Paint all the petals and allow
the first wash to dry. Then paint
a second layer near the tips of
the petals, blending out with a
damp, clean brush.

STEP 6

Let the petals dry, and repeat with a third layer of paint just at the tips of the petals.

STEP 7

Paint a light wash on all the inner areas of the mandala, leaving a small bit of white paper showing between each section. Paint a second and third layer near the tips of these shapes as you did on the smaller petals, blending the color out with water for each layer. Embellish with dots and lines.

CIRCLES MANDALA

Combine multiple circles in this pretty piece for a mesmerizing work of art. You can create this mandala with circles of any size. Use mine as inspiration, but as long as you are consistent with the circles on all four sides you can create any pattern you like!

MATERIALS
- Watercolor paper
- Compass with soft-lead pencil
- Watercolor paints
- Paintbrushes
- Blending stump

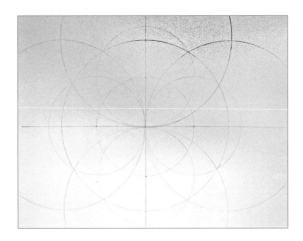

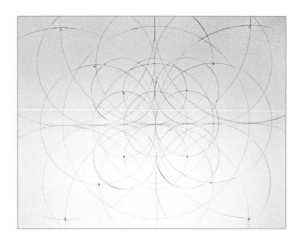

STEP 1

Follow steps 1 and 2 on page 25 to get started, filling about ¾ of the page with your initial circle. Once you have drawn four circles from the initial circle, adjust your compass to about half that width, and repeat these steps, starting at the center point again.

STEP 2

Adjust your compass again to about half of the width, and repeat, overlapping all of the different sizes of circles. To finish the drawing, make another circle at each of the dots shown, adjusting your compass to the previous widths. Remember that you don't have to follow my exact pattern—you may find it easier to create your own!

STEP 3

Select four petal shapes, and paint them as shown. I used shades of raw sienna, burnt umber, and yellow ochre.

STEP 4

Pick out any pattern you see in your drawing, and paint the details in a checkerboard pattern. Your pattern may look different than mine if you set up your circles differently.

STEP 5

Continue painting outward, filling open areas with one of the three main colors you started with.
When the paint is dry, trace the circles with a soft-lead pencil. Draw flourishes or other shapes in the open white spaces, as well as some of the painted spaces.

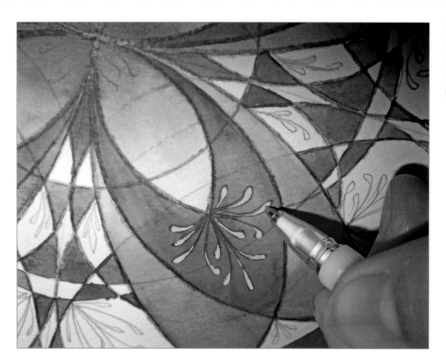

STEP 6

Use a white gel pen to fill in the details drawn in the watercolor segments.

STEP 7

Add a touch of watercolor paint (I used red) to the details drawn on the white segments.

PAPERCRAFT MANDALAS

MARISA EDGHILL

MAGICAL MANDALA CARDS

Just about everyone loves the simple pleasures of snail mail and stickers. Combine the two in mandala form, and the result is downright magical! These cheerful cards are perfect for thank you notes, get-well-soon sentiments, or simply saying hello. Make a stack, and send a little mandala magic out into the world. You can also use this technique to personalize notebooks and phone cases or create unique sticker art.

44

MATERIALS
- Butterfly stickers*
- Blank cards (5.5" square)
- Ruler or straight edge
- Pencil
- Eraser

  * Note: For each card, you will need about 20-24 stickers.

  Small stickers (approx. ½"-1") are easiest to work with.

STEP 1
Use a ruler or straight edge to lightly draw diagonal lines from the top corners to the bottom corners of the card.

STEP 2
Lightly draw a vertical line down the center of the card. Repeat with a horizontal line across the card.

STEP 3

Using the pencil lines as a guide, apply four matching stickers in a ring around the center of the card. Try to keep the spacing and positioning consistent.

STEP 4

Apply a second ring of stickers around the first. You should be able to fit eight stickers in this second round. Use eight of the same design or a mix of two different designs.

STEP 5
Continue adding stickers until the desired mandala
arrangement is achieved.

STEP 6
Carefully erase the pencil lines, and brush away the eraser dust. Your card is ready to send!

TRY SOMETHING DIFFERENT

Create your own mandala card designs by choosing stickers to match your personal taste. While butterflies are pretty, colorful fruit mandalas are a fresh take on this classic shape, and junk food versions are quirky-cute. When picking stickers, look for symmetrical shapes or sticker sets that include mirror images of the same design.

CUT-AND-PASTE COLLAGE MANDALA

Grab your glue and a stack of paper; with these simple materials, it's easy to create a layered mandala. Make it your own by mixing and matching different paper colors, patterns, and textures. Try creating a mandala out of painted patterns, bold-colored card stock, or even the pages of your favorite magazine. There's really no limit to the variations you can try.

MATERIALS
- Collage papers
- Templates (page 57)
- Scissors
- Paper
- Glue
- Circle punch (1/2" or 1", optional)
- Hole punch

Use collaging techniques to create stunning mandalas out of just about everything, including card stock, as pictured on page 42.

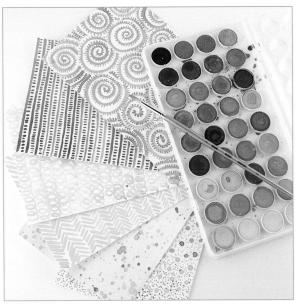

STEP 1
Collect or create the papers for your mandala. For this mandala, I chose to paint simple watercolor patterns for the different layers of the mandala.

STEP 2
Prepare the template. You can use the template shapes on page 57 or create your own shapes. (See Artist's Tip.)

ARTIST'S TIP

To create your own mandala template, cut a circle out of card stock. The size of the circle should be a little smaller than the desired mandala size. Determine how many points you'd like your mandala to have, and cut the circle into that number of wedges. Use each piece to design the different components of your mandala.

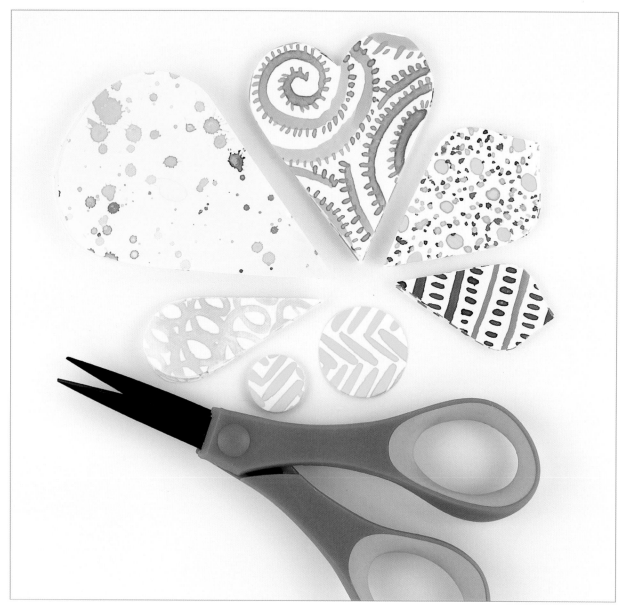

STEP 3

Cut out six pieces of each shape and one center circle.

STEP 4

Arrange the pieces into the desired layout. Once you are happy with the arrangement, it's time to start gluing.

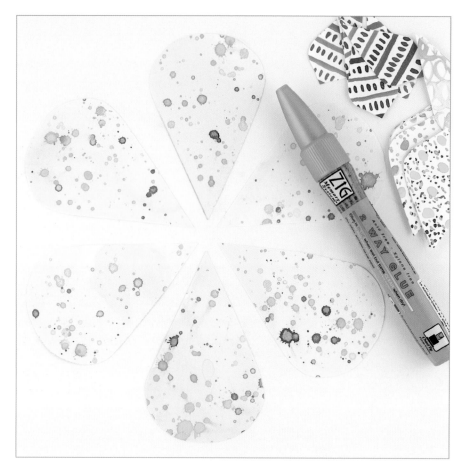

STEP 5
Glue the first six pieces to the paper in a circular formation, leaving a consistent amount of space between each piece (approximately ¼") and aligning the center points.

ARTIST'S TIP
Try using a glue pen instead of a glue stick. The marker-like applicator is easy to use and less messy than traditional glue sticks!

STEP 6
One layer at a time, continue gluing on the paper pieces.

STEP 7

Once all the pieces are glued, you can add small accent pieces to finish your design. A standard hole punch is fantastic for creating small circles.

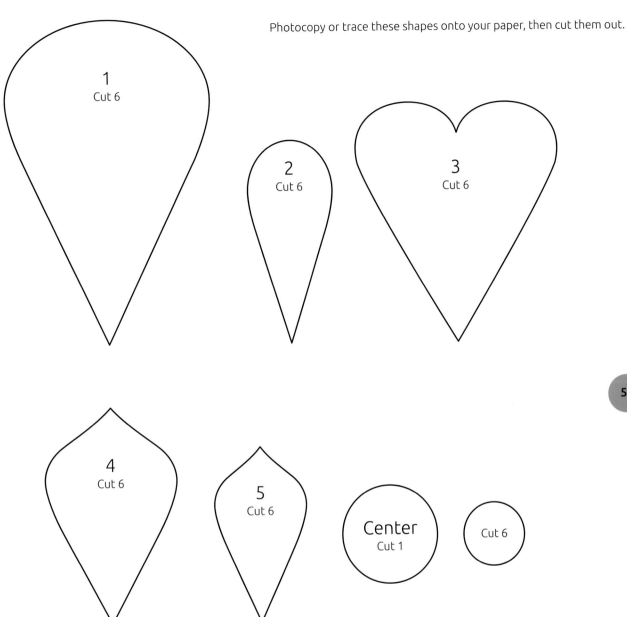

Photocopy or trace these shapes onto your paper, then cut them out.

1
Cut 6

2
Cut 6

3
Cut 6

4
Cut 6

5
Cut 6

Center
Cut 1

Cut 6

PAINTED PATTERNS

If you're looking for a relaxing art activity aside from mandalas, try painting simple watercolor patterns. Whether you choose a single color or a whole palette's worth, the repetitive action of pattern painting can be quite soothing once you get into the flow. Plus the finished patterns look beautiful framed or cut up for papercraft projects.

KIRIGAMI MANDALAS

The art of kirigami is one of my favorites. A few strategic folds and a handful of cuts creates beauty in everyday paper. While I've put together three templates for you to try, I think you'll enjoy the happy surprises in this style of paper cutting when you don't follow a set design. Fold, cut, and reveal something beautiful. I hope you love it as much as I do!

MATERIALS
- 6" (15cm) origami paper
- Scissors
- Templates (page 63)

STEP 1
Fold a piece of origami paper in half to form a triangle.
Then fold it in half again.

STEP 2
Position the paper triangle so that the center point
faces down. Fold the right third over the center third.

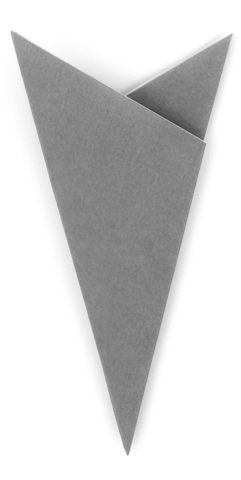

ARTIST'S TIP

Prefer to design your own kirigami mandala? Rather than unfolding the paper, simply sketch on your design or skip right to step 6 and start cutting.

STEP 4

Carefully unfold the paper. Position the triangular section you marked over the desired template on page 63. Lightly trace the design onto the paper.

STEP 3

Flip the paper over, and fold the remaining third, now positioned on the right, over the center third. Make a small pencil mark on the top triangle.

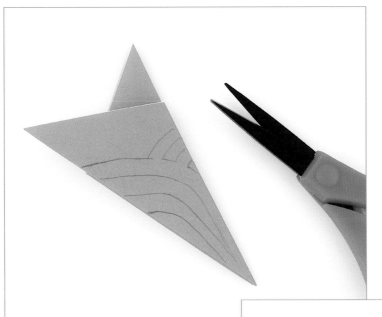

STEP 5
Refold the origami paper along the creases. Make sure that the triangle with the traced design ends up on top.

STEP 6
Cut your design. I find it easiest to start at the top and work my way down. Try to cut slightly on the inside of the traced lines to avoid pencil lines on your finished papercut.

61

STEP 7
Carefully unfold the
papercut to reveal your
kirigami mandala design.

KIRIGAMI TEMPLATES

Photocopy or trace these templates.

MAKE IT A FLOWER

Kirigami papercuts are infinitely adaptable. To transform the provided templates into flowers rather than mandalas, simply skip the two strips in the top right corner of each template. This simple adaptation allows you to cut striking kirigami flowers. Try adjusting the width and angle of the petals for a variety of flower shapes.

WASHI TAPE TREASURE BOX

Transform a boring blank box into a beautiful storage container, complete with a mandala design. Build a mandala out of colorful washi-tape shapes, while customizing the colors and design. Washi tape is a great multitasker that is ideal for art projects. You can easily reposition pieces for a stressless mandala-making experience. Washi tape mandalas can be created on anything you please—notebooks, walls, or even plain paper.

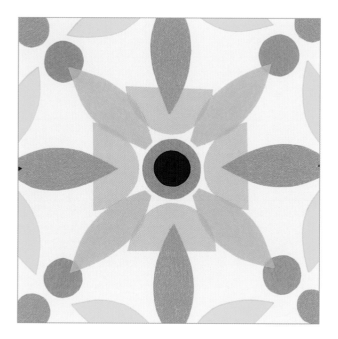

64

MATERIALS
- Square-lidded box
- Ruler
- Pencil
- Washi tape
- Backing paper (wax or parchment paper)
- Scissors
- Eraser

STEP 1

On the box lid, lightly draw a line from the top left corner to the bottom right corner. Repeat with a second line from the bottom left to the top right corner. Then draw a vertical line through the center point, followed by a horizontal line.

STEP 2

Apply strips of washi tape to your backing paper. Then cut out a variety of small shapes. For a four-point mandala, you will need four to eight pieces of each shape, except for the single center piece.

ARTIST'S TIP

Pencil marks will show through light colored washi tape. If any of your washi tape pieces overlap pencil lines, erase the lines a bit at a time as you apply tape pieces.

STEP 3
Arrange the shapes on the surface of the box lid. Try different layouts and cut any additional pieces you will need.

STEP 4

Once you are happy with the arrangement, begin peeling washi tape pieces off of their paper backings and sticking into position. Start at the middle, and work your way out. Erase all the pencil lines.

Apply washi tape stripes to the
body of the box and around
the rim of the box lid.

MAKE A MANDALA CANDLE

Create a simplified washi tape mandala on a glass candle holder. This pretty project makes a great gift or is perfect to help you relax.

FOUND MATERIALS
MANDALAS

ALYSSA STOKES

PHOTOGRAPHY & EDITING TECHNIQUES

Although it's awesome to see natural or found-object mandalas in real life, it is wonderful to be able to photograph and document your work. These images become lasting artwork. They are also a great way to share your art with others. You don't need fancy equipment or software—I typically photograph and edit my work with an iPhone®, although you can also use a DSLR camera and Adobe® Photoshop® or similar photo-editing software to create higher-resolution images.

SETTING UP THE STUDIO

Mandala-making doesn't require much space. All you need is a clear, flat surface—on the floor, a desk, or a table. I find working on a tabletop to be most comfortable, although it can limit the size of your mandala. Set up your workspace next to a window with plenty of natural light if possible. You will need several sheets of white or colored paper to use as backgrounds. I suggest purchasing a large sheet of white drawing paper, approximately 22" x 28", and several smaller sheets in various colors.

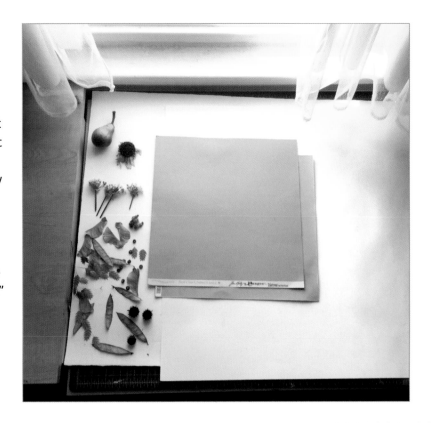

EDITING

In this example, I've demonstrated editing techniques on an iPhone®. You can achieve similar results with editing software on your own phone or a computer. Start by cropping and rotating the photograph to center the mandala. Then increase the exposure, contrast, brightness, and color saturation.

BEFORE

AFTER

I highly recommend Snapseed™, a free photo-editing application, to anyone serious about mobile photography. I like to use the "Selective" tool to brighten or adjust contrast and saturation in certain areas of the image. Snapseed also has a tool called "Spot Repair" that allows you to tap on the image to erase unwanted specks or marks—perfect for creating flawless imagery!

NATURE MANDALA WITH PRESSED FLOWERS

Pressing flowers is a great way to preserve and reuse your favorite natural objects in multiple mandala designs. Pressing also allows larger flowers to lay flat, acting as perfect mandala centers.

74

MATERIALS

- Cut flowers and small leaves
- Flower press or books
- Parchment paper
- Additional materials, such as beads and small stones*
- Scissors
- Tweezers

*Note: Collect materials that complement your flower focal point in color scheme.

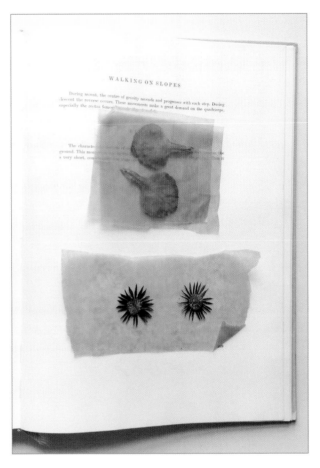

STEP 1

Press your flowers. You can purchase or build a flower press, but all you really need is wax or parchment paper and several heavy books. Place the flowers between two sheets of parchment paper near the back of a large book. Pile several other books on top and wait a few days.

ARTIST'S TIP

Ensure that the flower is spread flat when you place it in the press. It helps to trim off the stem first. More three-dimensional flowers can be taken apart before pressing and reassembled during the design process.

STEP 2

Arrange the first circular pattern around the pressed flower. Alternate between a natural object, such as a petal, and a circular object, such as a bead. Depending on the size of your objects, you may use 4-8 pieces of each small element.

STEP 3

Repeat with a second circle using different objects, such as leaves instead of petals. To complete your mandala, you may want to extend every other point further. For example, alternate between using a single petal and a leaf combined with a petal. Use tweezers to adjust the placement of your objects.

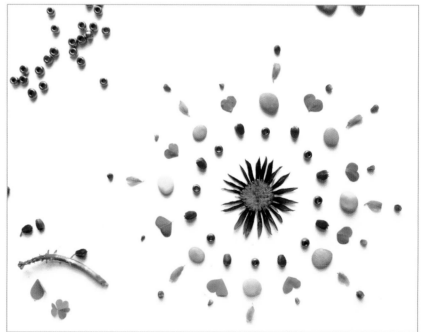

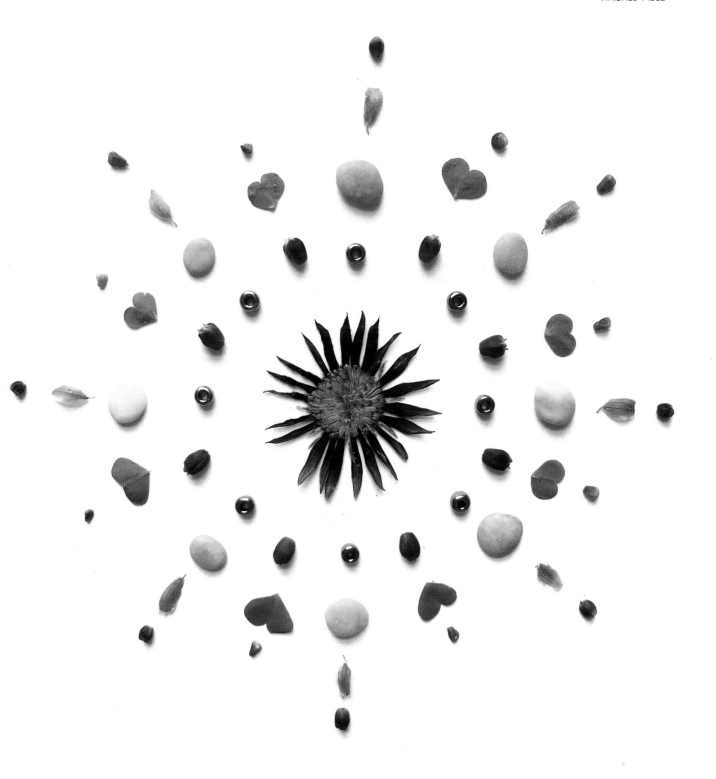

CANDY MANDALA

Candies—sweet and colorful delights—are perfect for crafting a bright and playful mandala.

MATERIALS
- Candy*
- White or colored paper
- Cutting board and knife (optional)

  *Note: I suggest purchasing at least six of each larger candy and a dozen of each smaller candy to maximize your options.

78

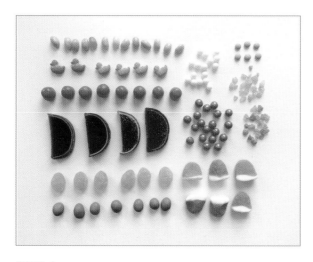

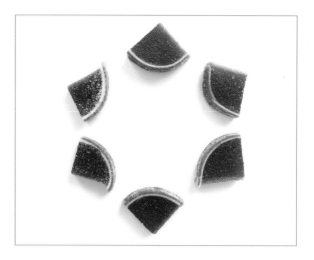

STEP 1
Lay out your candy on a clean surface—I prefer white—and sort by type, color, and size.

STEP 2
Begin with the largest candy that you would like to include in your mandala. Experiment with circular arrangements of four, six, or eight pieces.

STEP 3
Select and place a center focal point and some smaller candies inside the first candy ring.

STEP 5

Add two or more additional radial rings of candy. Consider creating a candy rainbow, or limit your color palette to shades of two or three colors.

ARTIST'S TIP

Repeat at least one type
of candy in a center ring
and an outer ring to bring
unity to your design.

SIMPLE GARDEN MANDALA

This easy-to-create garden mandala uses common weeds and wildflowers to create a sweet pastel design. It's a great mandala for beginners, and you can also repeat and build upon it to create more complex designs.

MATERIALS
- Cut flowers*
- Clover plant
- Small round objects
- Scissors
- Tweezers
- Color paint swatches (optional)

  *Note: Many flowers wilt quickly and must be used almost immediately after picking and not handled too much.

ARTIST'S TIP

Look for small flowers and weeds. Pick at least one type of flower, preferably something with small flat petals. Pick at least one clover plant, or something similar, with small green leaves.

STEP 1

Trim your flowers and clover plant, separating each petal and leaf. Save all parts of the flower—you may be able to use the pieces in your design. Lay out all of your mandala materials. Select a limited color palette, such as the pink and green that you see here. For the small round objects, I am using pink chocolate-covered sunflower seeds. You could use other types of small candies, buttons, stones, or beads.

83

STEP 2

Arrange four or five petals in a circular shape. Place the inside part of the flower, pistil, stamen, or other round object in the middle of the circle.

STEP 3

Select several clover leaves that are about the same size. Place them next to each petal, and use your tweezers to adjust the small leaves so that they all face outward.

STEP 4

Place small round objects or other flower parts in the spaces between each leaf. If you like, complement your simple mandala by placing paint swatches in similar colors next to or behind your design.

After photographing and editing your mandala, try making your own greeting cards by printing the image on card stock.

FOUND MATERIALS MANDALAS

BEACH MANDALA

This nature mandala is perfect for a summer trip to the beach, but you can create it any time of year using your shell collection and a little gathered sand.

MATERIALS
- Shells*
- Beach stones
- Sand

*Note: Collect multiples of the same type of shell; think in terms of three of a kind or more.

STEP 1

Organize your shells and stones, arranging the items by size and color. I grouped my shells into five sets of three, with three of the same general type, size, and color. Select a few more stones, 6 or 12 in a set, to fill in the mandala design.

STEP 2
Pour and pat the sand into a thin layer that covers an area approximately 12"x12", depending on the size of your shells. Work on a large sheet of white paper for easy cleanup! Create a natural looking edge to the sand by gradually thinning it out.

STEP 3

Select one unique shell for the focal point, and place it in the center of the sand circle. Then begin with two smaller shell sets. Arrange the shells evenly around the central focal point, alternating between the two types.

STEP 4

Continue to work out radially from the center point, by placing the next two sets of shells. Line up the outer shells with the inner ring of shells previously placed.

The Beach Mandala makes a great summer-themed centerpiece!

STEP 5

Place six of one type of stone between each shell in the inner ring. Then repeat this for the outer ring, using a different set of stones. If you wish, add more shells or stones to the outer ring of the mandala.

FOODIE MANDALA

This mandala can be created using your favorite recipe as inspiration or simply by raiding your refrigerator and choosing a colorful selection of fruits and veggies. A trip to the farmer's market is also a great starting point for this fresh twist on the found-object mandala!

MATERIALS
- Fruit (strawberries and lemon)
- Nuts or grains (sliced almonds)
- Kitchen knife
- Cutting board

STEP 1

Slice the fruit into round, even sections. Cut one of the citrus slices into four triangles. Cut at least two strawberries into triangular segments as well, by cutting off the top, slicing the fruit in half, and then cutting lengthwise.

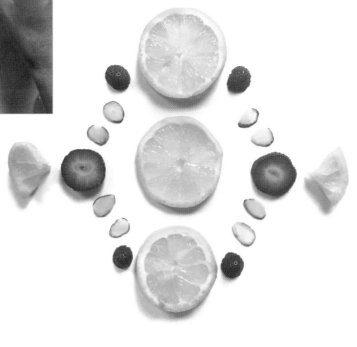

ARTIST'S TIP

Keep all of the cut pieces, including the tops of the strawberries.

STEP 2

Place the largest lemon segment in the center, with two similarly sized lemon sections above and below. Place two almond slices in the space between the lemons on the left and right sides. Place two larger strawberry slices, and two citrus triangles, on either side of the center lemon. Add two strawberry tips next to both the top and bottom lemons.

STEP 3

Add to the top and bottom of your design by placing the remaining two citrus triangles, pointing inward. Arrange four strawberry tops on each side of the lemon triangles. Outline the sections of your mandala with almond slices. Add four medium-size, circular strawberry slices to the left and right of the design.

STEP 4

Carefully pick the green leaves off of the tops of your remaining strawberries. Place a final large strawberry slice on the far left and right of your design. Surround each strawberry with five leaves and two small almond slices. Finish by creating a pointed crown on the top and bottom, using triangular strawberry slices (see "FINISHED PIECE").

Food mandalas are perfect for making your own recipe cards! They are also a great tool for encouraging young picky eaters to enjoy healthy snacks!

MANDALA INSPIRATION

If you look around, you can find materials for mandala making just about anywhere.

This walnut and cherry mandala utilizes a complementary color scheme.

Challenge yourself to pick just one color, and build a mandala using only items in that color.

You don't need sand to make a pretty beach mandala.

This mandala utilizes a neutral color scheme—it isn't necessary to use bright colors to create a beautiful mandala.

Notice how the light blue paper behind this mandala helps the colors "pop."

MIXED MEDIA MANDALAS

LOUISE GALE

WATERCOLOR BURSTS & GROWING A MANDALA DESIGN

Watercolor bursts can be a beautiful and fun way to create interesting colored backgrounds for mandala artwork. You can use just one color, or you can draw concentric circles, bursts, and patterns within a circular space using many different colors.

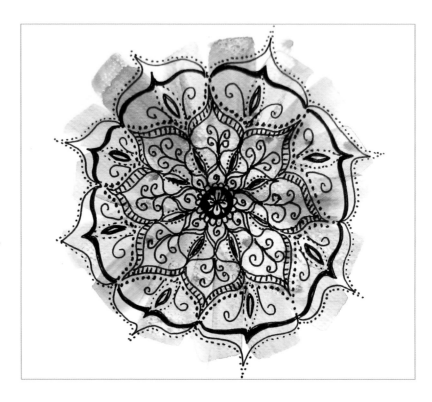

MATERIALS
- Watercolor paper
- Watercolor paints
- Paintbrushes
- Fine-tipped black pen or marker

STEP 1
Load a medium flat brush with watercolor paint. Imagine a center point, and paint thick lines from the center outward, creating an eight-point star. I like to leave some white space so I can add another color, but you can paint as many lines as you like, depending on the size of your brush and number of colors you wish to use.

STEP 2
Choose another color and paint between the first lines, overlapping the colors. You will start to see interesting layers and pattern appear as you add more color.

101

STEP 3
While the paint is wet, dot a new color of paint over the bursts; this will create additional patterns as the paint sinks into the wet background.

ARTIST'S TIP
Use a variety of brush sizes to create interesting patterns on your watercolor burst.

STEP 4

While the paint is wet, place another sheet of paper on it to blot the paint. This will create a mirrored "ghost print," which you can use later for another mandala project.

STEP 5

Let dry. Then draw a dot or a small flower at the center. From here, you will grow your mandala using your favorite motifs and designs. See "My Motifs" for the designs I'm using in this mandala. Start with your favorite motif, and let your intuition guide you.

ARTIST'S TIP

Create a variety of watercolor bursts on separate sheets of paper, using an array of colors, for more mandala art using this technique.

MY MOTIFS

STEP 6
For the next layer, draw petals or shapes using eight points. Draw four petals first (as in north, south, east, and west); then add the next four in between. The beauty of creating a mandala this way is that it is not perfectly symmetrical and is more organic in shapes and sizes.

STEP 7
Use the tips of the petals or your shape as a guide to draw and repeat your next motif in between the existing shapes, building the mandala outward. Fill in any spaces with little squiggles, leaves, or floral elements.

STEP 8
Keep growing your mandala, adding another layer around the outside of your existing drawing.

STEP 9
Add as many layers as you would like until you reach the edge of the watercolor burst or decide your mandala is finished.

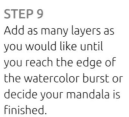

CREATIVE TIPS

- You can also use other paints, such as acrylic, to create the same effect.
- Make color copies of your bursts before you draw on them to use in other mixed media mandala projects.
- Doodle your mandala using different colored pens.

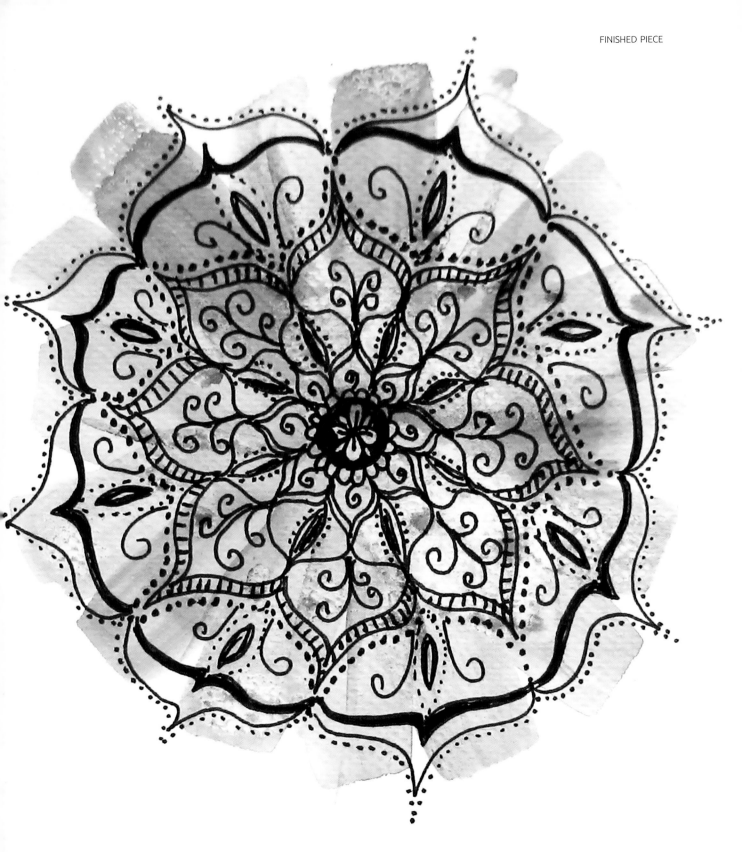

ALCOHOL INKS ON WOOD

Create a beautiful background for your mandala artwork using alcohol inks on wood.

MATERIALS
- Plywood panel
- Alcohol inks* in various colors
- Water jar
- Water spray bottle (optional)
- Foam brush or regular wide brush
- Metallic acrylic paints and pens
- Compass and pencil
- Black pen
- White paint pen or gel pen

  * Note: If you do not have alcohol inks, use regular ink or watercolor paints to stain the wood.

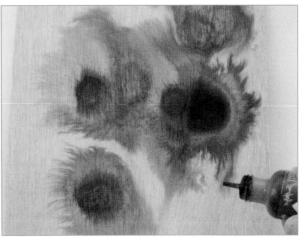

STEP 1
Wet the surface of a plywood panel with water, using a large foam or regular paintbrush.

STEP 2
Choose one ink for the base color, and gently squeeze drops of ink onto the wood. The wet surface immediately soaks up the ink and creates interesting patterns that burst outward across the panel.

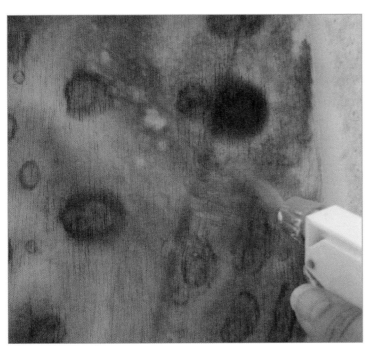

STEP 3
Experiment with different levels of pressure as you squeeze the bottle, and move your hand around to create patterns. To spread the base color, use a spray bottle of water to spread the ink to cover all of the exposed wood.

ARTIST'S TIP
You may find that the vibrancy of color fades a little as the ink sinks into the wood and dries, so don't be shy about using vibrant, deep colors.

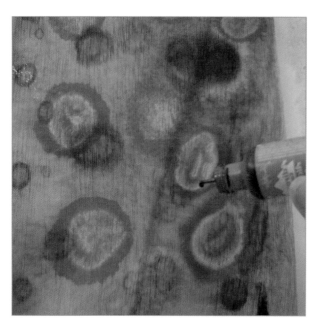

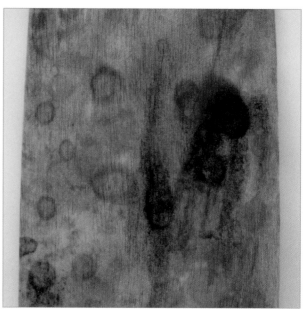

STEP 4

While the ink is still wet, add more colors to the panel. With the wet surface, more interesting color mixtures and patterns will emerge. You can even try dripping or stroking the color on to create different shapes.

STEP 5

Use a rubber stamp or your fingers to create shapes and dots in areas that need more detail, letting your intuition guide you. Let the finished background dry. If the wood is thin, you may need to place it under a heavy book to prevent warping.

ARTIST'S TIP

To create patterns in the background, you can also use a cork, the end of your paintbrush, or the rim of a bottle top.

STEP 6

Now you're ready to add your mandala. Get started using a compass and pencil to draw concentric circles to create a guide. If you want to create more emphasis, use a thicker pen to draw over the lines.

STEP 7

For this mandala, I started with four points in the center to create a lotus petal. Then I added another four points and drew the additional four petals overlapping in the center. Draw your motifs with a pencil if you are unsure what colors you want to add at this stage, or go for it with a black or colored pen.

STEP 8

Continue to draw your motifs around the next circle. Fill in the center. Here I have used gold acrylic paint and a white paint pen.

STEP 9

Continue to add detail, layering over the paint with a white paint pen, creating outlines, dots, and detail to help the design "pop." Work all the way out to complete your mandala.

HENNA-INSPIRED MANDALA

Henna body painting (also known as "Mehndi") is an art form that has been practiced in India for many years. It comes from the henna plant and is traditionally used for weddings and other occasions. Many mandala artists use this art form as inspiration for motifs and mandala creation. In this project, you will be inspired to collect your own motifs to create a mandala wall hanging.

MATERIALS
- Plaster of Paris® bandage roll*
- Cardboard
- Compass and pencil
- Scissors
- Tape
- Plaster gauze strips
- Small bowl of warm water
- Ribbon
- Henna pen or brown felt-tip/paint pen

* Note: It's important to handle plaster of paris carefully and with adult supervision. Avoid getting it in your eyes or inhaling it. Wear eye protection, gloves and a mask if necessary. Be sure to read the label before using.

113

STEP 1

Before you get started, find henna and Mehndi art inspiration. Try designing your own motifs you can use in your mandala. Here are just a few motifs I found for inspiration.

STEP 2

Cut different sizes of circles out of cardboard.

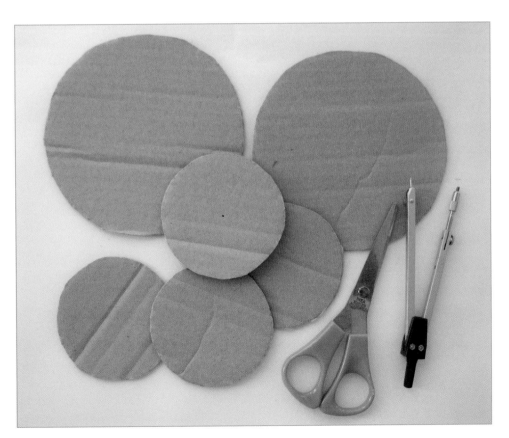

STEP 3

Tape a piece of ribbon to one side of a circle to create the hanging element. Run a strip of plaster gauze through the bowl of warm water for a few seconds. Place it on the cardboard, and use your finger to flatten and smooth out the plaster; it will adhere itself to the cardboard. Then wrap the edges around to secure it to the back.

STEP 4

Continue to wet and add strips to the circle. Two layers should be enough. Then turn it over to cover the back. It doesn't need to be perfectly flat; this adds to the plaster effect and handmade element of the mandala. Repeat this process with the other circles.

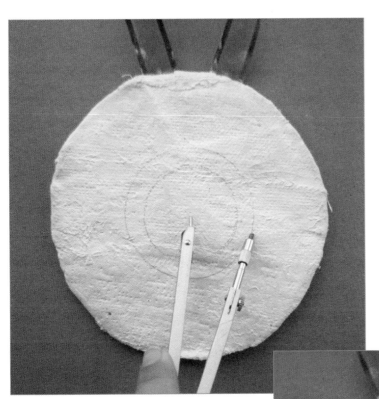

STEP 5
Once your plaster circles are dry, lightly pencil concentric circles on the plaster to use as a guide.

STEP 6
Refer back to your motifs for inspiration, and start in the center with one main motif, such as a lotus flower.

ARTIST'S TIP

Use real henna in a tube to create a more authentic, embossed look in your mandala design.

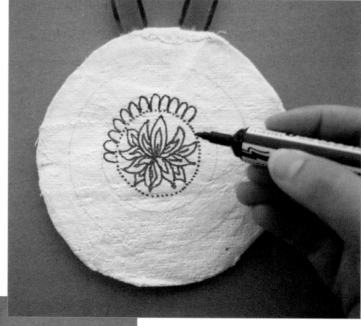

STEP 7

Continue working on the design of the first circle. This may include dots, a lined circle, and a repeated motif to frame the center.

STEP 8

Working your way out, add elements and motifs to grow the mandala design.

MIXED MEDIA MANDALA ON CANVAS

Mixed media mandalas are so much fun—you can use so many different materials, and the result is always stunning. Follow this step-by-step process to create one on canvas that you can hang on your wall and enjoy.

MATERIALS
- Square, stretched canvas (any size)
- Acrylic paint
- Spray paint (optional)
- India ink and water-soluble crayons (optional)
- Paintbrushes or roller
- Collage papers
- Stencils or doilies
- Compass and ruler
- Pens (including gel pens and ink pens)

STEP 1
Using the color of your choice, brush or roll acrylic paint onto the canvas to create a base color. Keep it uneven to create interesting texture.

STEP 2
Gather stencils and items you can use to create pattern, such as a doily. Create the first layer of pattern using spray paint or by dabbing on paint with a brush. Use a contrasting color—metallic paint works well. *Note: If using spray paint, work outdoors or in a well-ventilated room.*

STEP 3
Repeat with a different stencil to create a second layer with another contrasting color. You can also try using small parts of the stencil rather than the whole stencil for different effects.

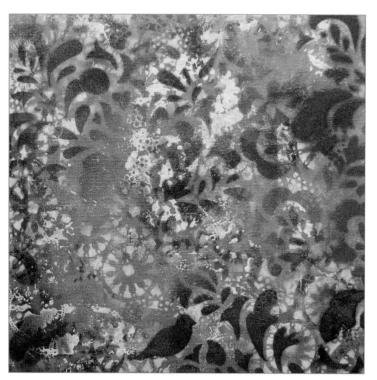

STEP 4

Continue building up the layers until you are happy with the background. I added an additional layer of white and purple spray paint to mine.

ARTIST'S TIP

Laying tissue paper over the background will let it show through, creating a transparent effect around the edges of the design.

STEP 5

Add any additional elements to the background, such as collage or tissue paper. Then use a compass to draw concentric circles as guide for drawing your mandala. Outline the circles with a gel pen.

STEP 6

Start at the center and use the 8-point method to draw petal shapes in the first circle. Work your way outward, connecting the tip of the previous petal with the new petal. (See sketch.) In this mandala, the lotus petal shape is repeated throughout the design; choose a motif to repeat, or use a variety of motifs.

MIXED MEDIA MANDALAS

STEP 7

Once you have completed the outlines, start to color in the petals using inks, acrylic paint, or other mediums. Work outward to avoid smudging.

STEP 8

If your background is very busy the mandala can become lost in it. To help the mandala "pop," use a white water-soluble crayon or transparent paint to lightly fill in the other areas of the mandala, defining the mandala design but letting the background still peek through.

STEP 9

Outline the mandala by drawing around the outer circle with the crayon or gel pen. Then continue to fill in the other areas of the mandala to further define the design, still allowing some of the detail from the background to show through. Create a series of dots or arches around the outer circle to finish the mandala (see "FINISHED PIECE").

ABSTRACT MANDALA COLLAGES

Collage can be lots of fun, and creating basic mandalas is very calming as you allow your intuition to guide you with papers and glue.

MATERIALS
- Collage papers
- Paint
- Paintbrushes
- Jar of water
- Scissors
- Glue

STEP 1

Paint a circle on a piece of paper. While the paint is wet, gently press another piece of paper on top to create a "ghost print."

STEP 2

Gather some collage materials—this can include other painted circles, tissue paper, collage paper, etc.

STEP 3

Cut out paper shapes to use for the collage, such as a circle for the center, leaf shapes, or curved paper pieces.

STEP 4

You can build your mandala around the painted circle or the ghost image. Begin to place and glue the collage pieces. I've used my curved paper shapes to create a swirling water effect.

STEP 5
Add additional elements with pen or paint, such as small doodles or motifs in the mandala or petals around the edges.

There are endless ways to build abstract collage mandalas.
Try this technique, and then come up with some of your own.

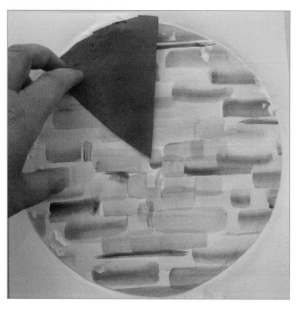

Try painting your own papers to use as a background or as pieces in the collage.

Cut collage papers into pie-piece shapes and glue them to the base.

Add more layers in different textures and tones until you're happy with the effect. Cover the center points with another circle, if you like.

ABOUT THE AUTHORS

Marisa Edghill is a Canadian craft designer, writer, and paper artist. Known for her work with washi tape and kirigami papercutting, Marisa delights in transforming ordinary materials into something beautiful. She shares art projects and plenty of crafty inspiration on her website www.omiyageblogs.ca. Marisa is the author of *Paper + Tape: Craft & Create* (Walter Foster, 2016), *Washi Style* (St Martin's Press, 2015) and contributing author to *Pinterest Perfect!* (Walter Foster, 2014).

Louise Gale is a British mixed media artist, passionate about color, nature, and mandala making. She paints and runs online workshops from her Spanish art studio overlooking the sea. With a fascination for crop circles, sacred geometry, and patterns in nature, Louise loves to explore creative possibilities within the sacred circle—from mandalas in nature and intuitive doodles to large, mixed media, mandala masterpieces.

Alyssa Stokes is a Baltimore artist and art educator. She is greatly influenced by nature, and her work includes nautical and woodland altered photographs, as well as various still life petal plays.

Andrea Thompson is an artist who squeezes in time to create whenever she can, working mostly in watercolor. She loves nature, the river, and contrast of white on white patterns, and color.